P9-DEP-210

Fun With GRAMMAR

by Laura Sunley

SCHOLASTIC
PROFESSIONAL BOOKS

New York • Toronto • London • Auckland • Sydney
Mexico City • New Delhi • Hong Kong • Buenos Aires

Scholastic Inc. grants teachers permission to photocopy the reproducible pages
from this book for classroom use. No other part of this publication may be
reproduced in whole or in part, or stored in a retrieval system, or transmitted
in any form or by any means, mechanical, photocopying, recording, or otherwise,
without written permission of the publisher. For information regarding permission,
write to Scholastic Inc., 557 Broadway, New York, NY 10012.

Edited by Kathleen Fitzgibbon
Cover design by Pamela Simmons
Cover illustrations by Mike Moran
Interior design by Sydney Wright
ISBN 0-439-28234-9

Copyright © 2002 by Laura Sunley.
All rights reserved.
Printed in the U.S.A.

8 9 10   40   09 07 06

Contents

Introduction

Can teaching grammar be fun? Yes, when children are excited and enjoy what they are doing. Encouraging children to brainstorm, write, research, and work together creates an enriching environment for learning. Synthesizing knowledge of the parts of speech and showing students how they can use that information is an effective educator's goal.

This book has easy and fun hands-on activities, cooperative games, and writing ideas. They create a spark of interest in students. I hope that your children enjoy them as much as mine do.

Using the Book

Each section opener of the book includes a page with a definition of a part of speech. You may want to create an overhead transparency of the page. You can read through the definition with your class, and work with them to complete the lists of examples. It may be helpful to keep the page displayed as students play the games or complete the activities related to each part of speech.

Nouns

A **noun** is a word that names a person, place, thing, or idea. A noun can act or be acted upon.

A **common noun** is a general name for a person, place, or thing.

A **proper noun** names a specific person, place, or thing. Proper nouns are often made up of more than one word. Proper nouns are usually capitalized.

The following is a list of examples of common and proper nouns. Complete the list with your own common and proper nouns.

COMMON NOUN	PROPER NOUN
boy	Carlos
astronaut	Sally Ride
country	India
day	Thursday
month	May
river	Mississippi
state	Wyoming
author	J. K. Rowling
park	Bryce Canyon National Park
inventor	Alexander Graham Bell
teacher	_____
city	_____
_____	Abraham Lincoln
_____	Statue of Liberty
_____	_____
_____	_____

Brainstorm!

Materials

newspapers, old magazines, scissors, glue

Directions

Working in pairs, have students look through old newspapers and magazines to find examples of nouns. Have them cut out the nouns and glue them to chart paper. Have each pair find two examples each of a person, a place, a thing, and an idea. Once each group has contributed eight nouns, review the words with the group to determine that each word is an example of a noun.

Variation

Have students find examples of common nouns and proper nouns. Have them create two brainstormed lists by gluing the words to a common noun list and a proper noun list.

I Know That Story!

Materials

simple picture book with words

Directions

Explain to students that you will read them a story. Tell them to listen for proper nouns in the story. When they hear a proper noun, they should raise their hands.

Variation

Have students stand when they hear a proper noun and raise their hands when they hear a common noun.

Tip

This game provides students with practice with proper nouns. You may wish to use page 6 to review the definition of a proper noun and review the examples of proper nouns.

Switch!

Materials

paper, pencil

Directions

Have each student write a list of five common nouns. Then have the students switch papers with a partner. The partner then writes a proper noun example for each common noun listed. Pairs switch papers with another pair to check that each word is an example of a common or proper noun.

Variation

Students first write proper nouns and partners provides common nouns.

What Is Your Favorite?

Materials

butcher paper, highlighter markers in two colors, paper, pencils

Directions

Draw a tally chart on butcher paper. Poll the students as to their favorite form of entertainment. Include activities such as watching television, reading books, going to the movies, and listening to music. Tally their responses on a class chart. Have students list nouns related to their favorite form of entertainment. Then, have them exchange lists with a partner and highlight each proper noun with one highlighter and the common nouns using the other highlighter.

Variations

◆ Let students who have the same favorite form of entertainment compare noun lists to see how many of the same nouns they both selected.

◆ Have students use their noun lists to write a brief description of their favorite form of entertainment.

✦ 5 ✦
Don't Say It

Directions

One student is chosen to be the Don't Say It tester. He or she goes around the room asking questions that try to trick the other players into saying a proper noun. Any player who uses a proper noun is eliminated. The game continues until one player is left. That player then gets to be the tester. For example, the tester asks, "Where were you born?" "Which hospital were you born in?" or "What is your birthday?"

Variation

Players cannot respond using common nouns. This variation is more difficult so you may want to allow each player to say three common nouns before he or she is eliminated.

✦ 6 ✦
Quiz Show

Materials

game board, category clues (see below)

Make a game board by laminating ten envelopes and cutting them in half to create 20 pockets. Leave space at the top of the game board for category titles to be added. Glue the pockets onto poster board to make four columns of five pockets. Label each pocket in each column with a point value. The top row of pockets should be labeled 5, the next row should be labeled 10, and so on (see photo). Once you've decided on categories, write clues for each category on index cards.

Directions

Write the following category names on index cards: *Proper Nouns*, *Plural Nouns*, *Noun or Not?* and *Common Nouns*.

Attach the cards to the top of each column on the game board using paper clips. For *Proper Nouns*, the student will provide a proper noun for a common noun given on an index card. An example of a common noun would be *singer* or *holiday*. For *Plural Nouns*, the student will spell the plural form of a common noun. For *Noun or Not?*, the student will say whether a word is a noun or not. For *Common Nouns*, the student will provide two common nouns related to a category. An example of a category would be *school building*.

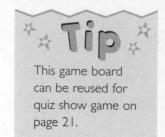

Tip

This game board can be reused for quiz show game on page 21.

The game is played by two contestants. The first contestant selects a category and an amount of points. He or she reads the clue aloud. If the other contestant responds correctly to the clue, he or she is awarded the points. If the contestant responds incorrectly, the points are deducted from his or her score. Each contestant takes a turn reading and answering a question until the board is cleared. The player with the most points wins.

Variations

◆ Play the game with teams instead of individual players.

◆ Let small groups of students write the clues.

7
Tic-Tac-Toe

Materials

reproducible on page 53

Directions

Distribute a copy of the Tic-Tac-Toe reproducible to pairs of students. Explain to students that instead of using *Xs* and *Os*, one student will use common nouns and one will use proper nouns. For example, the first player writes a common noun in one square on the grid. The second player writes a proper noun in another square on the grid. The first player to write three in a row—across, up and down, or diagonally—is the winner. Students should check their words for proper capitalization.

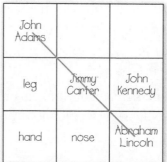

Variation

One student writes singular nouns and one writes plural nouns.

⟨8⟩
Categories

Materials ✳

reproducible on page 53; reference books such as an atlas, almanac, dictionary, and encyclopedia

Directions ✳

Let students brainstorm a list of noun categories. Remind them that the categories should be people (such as *boys' names* or *politicians*), places (such as *state, city*), things (such as *toys* or *vegetables*). Pick four categories from the list to have students write at the top of each column. Then, choose five letters for them to write in the first column. Explain to students that they should try to fill in the grid with nouns that belong in the category and start with the letter in the first column. Students may use reference books to find nouns. When grids are complete, let students share answers in a small group. Students should applaud any unusual or unique answers.

Tip

Categories can be played by individuals, pairs, small groups, or the whole class.

⟨9⟩
Noun Safari

Materials ✳

sticky note paper in three different colors

Directions ✳

To help students understand just how many different nouns there are, tell them they will label all the nouns they can find in your classroom. Divide the class into small groups. Assign each group a section of the classroom. Provide each group with sticky notes in three different colors: one for people, one for places, and one for things. Then have students "go on safari," finding and labeling the nouns they see. Have each group tell about the nouns they found. The group with the most nouns is the winner.

Variation ✳

This activity can also be used with magazine and book illustrations. Have students label the nouns they find in the pictures.

{10} Alphabet Soup

Materials

alphabet cards (each card has one letter of the alphabet)

Directions

Each student should select one alphabet card. Have them answer the following questions with fictitious answers. Each answer must begin with their chosen letter.

1. Who are you? (*person*)   2. Where are you? (*place*)
3. What is in your hand? (*thing*)   4. What are you thinking? (*idea*)

Then have them use their answers to write a short story.

1. Henry   2. Honolulu
3. hot dog   4. how hot it is

Henry stood on the sidewalk in downtown Honolulu holding a hula hoop. "It sure is hot," Henry thought.

Henry turned to his friend Hank and said, "Let's go to the beach and cool off. We can get hot dogs there."

That's when their adventure began.

Variation

Have students read their stories aloud and let the group guess what letter that student chose.

{11} Metaphorically Speaking

Materials

sentence strips

Directions

Review metaphors with students by reminding them that a metaphor is a literary device that compares two things, but does not use the words *like* and *as*. Write the following metaphors on sentence strips and display them for students to see:

Tip

Use the sentence strips and illustrations as a bulletin board display.

> That telephone is an old dinosaur.
> Her brain is a regular adding machine!
> The hungry boy's stomach was a bottomless pit.
> I am a real chicken when it comes to getting a shot.

Have students identify what kinds of nouns are in each metaphor. Underline the nouns. Working in small groups, have students write two metaphors on sentence strips. Have them underline the nouns in each. Display the sentence strips. Let each student select one metaphor to illustrate.

Verbs

A **verb** is a word that shows action, being, or a state of being.
An **action verb** expresses action.
A **state-of-being verb** shows that someone or something *is*. A state-of-being verb does not show action.

The following is a list of sentences with examples of action verbs and state-of-being verbs. Complete the list with your own action and state-of-being verbs.

ACTION VERBS	STATE-OF-BEING VERB
Cody *studied* for the test.	Cody *is* a quiet child.
Kisha and Rachel *swam* to the raft.	Kisha and Rachel *are* swimmers.
The cat *looked* down the alley.	The cat *was* careful.
The boys *danced* across the stage.	_____
_____	They *are* brother and sister.

☆12☆
Brainstorm!

Materials

newspapers, old magazines, scissors, glue

Directions

Working in pairs, have students look through old newspapers and magazines to find five examples of action verbs. Have them cut out the verbs and glue them to chart paper. Once each group has contributed five verbs, review the words with the group and let students pantomime each action.

Variations

◆ Have students find examples of action verbs and state-of-being verbs. Have them create two brainstormed lists by gluing the words to an action verb list and a state-of-being verb list.

◆ Have one group find present-tense verbs, and the other group find past-tense verbs. Let volunteers use each word in a sentence.

☆13☆
Verb Detective

Materials

simple picture book with words

Directions

Explain to students that you will read them a story. Tell them to listen for action verbs in the story. When they hear an action verb, they should raise their hands.

Variation

◆ Have students stand when they hear an action verb and raise their hands when they hear a state-of-being verb.

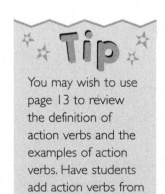

Tip

You may wish to use page 13 to review the definition of action verbs and the examples of action verbs. Have students add action verbs from the story to their lists.

Linking Verbs Paper Chain

Materials

construction paper in a variety of colors, pens, scissors, rulers

Directions

To help students remember that some verbs are linking verbs, have them make linking verb paper chains. First brainstorm a list of linking verbs and then write them on chart paper or the chalkboard. Have students cut the construction paper horizontally into 2-inch wide strips. Have them write linking verbs on the strips and then roll, link, and tape them to make paper chains. Use the colorful chains to decorate your classroom.

Let's Play Charades

Materials

index cards and writing materials

Directions

Distribute one card to each student. Have each student write an action verb on the card. Place the cards in a hat or box. Have students form two teams. The first player draws a card from the hat and must act the word out without speaking. The player's teammates must guess the verb within a two-minute time period. If the team guesses the correct word, they receive a point. Play continues with a player from the second team. Each team in turn acts out a word until all word cards have been used. The team with the most points wins.

✨ 16 ✨
Dictionary Double Check

Materials ✳

dictionary, timer or clock with a second hand, paper, pencils

Directions ✳

Choose one student to be the timekeeper. The timekeeper chooses a letter of the alphabet. They can do this by opening a book with their eyes closed and pointing to a page. The letter pointed to is the letter chosen (exclude *k, q, x*). The timekeeper announces that letter and starts the timer. All students have two minutes to write as many verbs as possible that start with that letter. For example, if the selected letter is *h*, students may list *hit, hurt, hurry, hug*.

When time is up, students use their dictionaries to check spelling and the part of speech. You may wish to remind students that dictionaries show the part of speech in italics after the word (it may be spelled out or abbreviated *v.*). The student who correctly wrote the most verbs becomes the timekeeper for the next round.

Variation ✳

◆ Have students write a list of verbs that contain the selected letter. The word does not have to start with the letter. For example, if the selected letter is *p*, students may list *play, park, clap, apply*, or *rap*.

✨ 17 ✨
Don't Say It/Say It

Directions ✳

One student is chosen to be the Don't Say It/Say It tester. He or she goes around the room asking questions that try to trick the other players into saying a verb. Any player who uses a verb is eliminated. The game continues until one player is left. That player then gets to be the tester. For example, the tester asks, "What are you doing? How did you get to school? What do you like to do at recess?"

Play the game again, only this time players must respond to a question with a verb. If they say a noun, they are eliminated.

{18}

Make a Movie!

Materials

reproducible on page 54, scissors, oak tag, paste, tape, colored pencils, crayons or colored pens

Directions

Distribute a copy of the Movie Frames reproducible to pairs of students. Instruct them to cut out the movie strips along the bottom of the page. Have them tape the strips together to make a six-frame movie. Have them cut out the theater and paste it onto a piece of oak tag cut to size. Tell them to carefully cut along the inner solid lines to make a cutaway box (the movie screen) with two slits running alongside it.

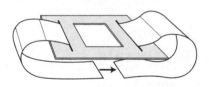

Explain to students that they are going to make an action-adventure movie. The first box is the title frame for the movie. They should write and illustrate an action-adventure movie in the rest of the frames. Challenge students to use as many action verbs as they can in their movies.

Students "show" their movies by threading the long strip through the slits on the movie screen. They should align the free ends of the strip and tape them together to create one continuous loop. Have them pull the strip to the left until the movie title is visible through the cutaway screen. To view the movie, they should pull the strip to the left, box by box.

{19}

Imagination

Materials

recordings of music that express aspects of nature, such as *Grand Canyon Suite* by Ferde Grofé, *Appalachian Spring* by Aaron Copland, *Nature's Symphonies—Rain Forest*, or many meditation tapes; paper; crayons or colored pencils; red and blue markers

Directions

Turn the lights down low. Have students get comfortable. Then play a nature recording. Have students close their eyes and

listen. Have each student draw pictures of the images that come to mind as they listen to the music. Have them label the pictures with a subject and action verb. Have them underline the subject in blue and the verb in red. Let students share their pictures and labels with the class.

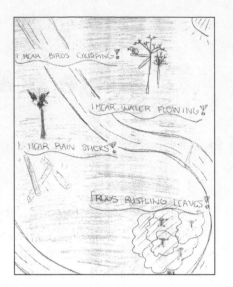

Tip

This makes a great hall display.

20
Animal Poems

Materials

drawing paper, markers, construction paper

Directions

Students should pick an animal or character they like to draw. Have them draw and color the animal on drawing paper. On another piece of paper, have them respond to the question "What can this animal do?" with action verbs. Tell them to write the verbs into phrases to make a poem. Have them copy the poem onto the drawing of the animal. Encourage students to underline each verb in red. Let students cut out the animal and mount it on construction paper. Have them write the title for their poem on the construction paper.

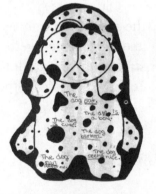

Tip

Have students trim the construction paper, leaving a one-inch border. These make a great display!

Adjectives

An **adjective** is a word that modifies or describes a noun or a pronoun. It can tell what kind, how many, or which one.

A, *an*, and *the* are adjectives that are called **articles**. A and *an* are used before singular nouns. A is used before words that begin with a consonant sound. *An* is used before words that begin with a vowel sound. *The* is used before singular and plural nouns.

The following is a list of examples of adjectives. Complete the list with your own adjectives.

What Kind?	How Many?	Which One?
blue sweater	**two** basketballs	**that** puddle
huge elephant	**some** people	**the red** one
Mexican flag	**few** coins	**those** clothes
_____ restaurant	_____ friends	_____ cat
_____ child	_____ classrooms	_____ dachshunds
_____ sky	_____	_____
_____	_____	_____
_____	_____	_____
_____	_____	_____
_____	_____	_____

☆21☆
That Star Is . . .

Materials

8½- by 11-inch sheet of blank white paper, magazines and newspapers, tape or glue

Directions

Have students cut out a star shape from the paper. Then have students find and cut out a picture of a famous musician, singer, or actor. Have them glue or tape the picture to the middle of the star (or they may want to draw the person). Ask students to write a list of adjectives to describe the person they selected around the picture. Have students share their lists in small groups. Let the group members evaluate whether the words are adjectives or not.

Variations

◆ Let students use their adjective list to write a descriptive paragraph about the person.
◆ Display a work of art such as a well-known painting. Have students write adjectives to describe the painting.
◆ Hold up an object such as a flower for students to use to brainstorm adjectives.

☆22☆
Once Upon a Time

Materials

reproducible on page 55, or copies of tales you are reading in your class

Directions

Distribute copies of the tales to pairs of students. Have students complete the stories by adding adjectives. Invite students to read their completed tales aloud.

Variation

◆ Use literature your class is studying.

Adjective Bingo

Materials

reproducible on page 56, markers such as beans or buttons, list of 24 adjectives on chart paper or the board

Directions

Distribute one copy of the *Bingo* reproducible to each student. Display the list of 24 adjectives. Instruct students to fill in the spaces on their *Bingo* cards, in any order, with the adjectives. Possible adjectives:

orange	large	sticky	American	all	pink
some	fourteen	second	that	this	sunny
lightest	heavier	best	better	none	hard
ugly	gorgeous	awesome	amazing	sad	smooth

Then, say a fill-in-the-blank sentence to the class. As you read, students place a marker on the adjective that would complete the sentence correctly. The first player to score five words in a row— horizontally, vertically, or diagonally—wins the game. Check students' work to be sure they chose an adjective that makes sense to complete the sentence.

Variation

◆ Let students play until someone covers an "I" formation on their card, or play with an "H" formation as the goal.

24
Quiz Show

Materials

game board (see page 9 for directions), index cards with clues for each category (see below)

Directions

Write the following category names on index cards and attach them with paper clips to the top of each column on the game board: *How Many?, Comparative Adjective, Superlative Adjective, Article, Demonstrative Adjective*. Then write clue sentences for each category. For example, for the category *How Many?*, the student will use an adjective that tells how many correctly in a sentence.

For *Comparative Adjective*, the student changes the adjective into a comparative adjective and uses it in a sentence. For *Superlative Adjective*, the student changes the adjective into a superlative adjective and uses it in a sentence. For *Article*, the student chooses the correct article to complete the sentence. For *Demonstrative Adjective*, the student points to an object and uses a demonstrative adjective to tell a sentence about the object.

The game is played by three contestants. The first contestant selects a category and an amount of points. If the contestant responds correctly to the clue, he or she is awarded the points. If the contestant responds incorrectly, the points are deducted from his or her score. Each contestant takes a turn answering a question until the board is cleared. The player with the most points wins.

Variations

◆ Play the game with teams instead of individual players.

◆ Let small groups of students write the clues.

25

I Can Beat That Word

Materials

reproducible on page 57, thesauruses, pencils

Directions

Review with students how to use a thesaurus before beginning this activity. Divide the class into six groups. Distribute one *I Can Beat That Word* reproducible to each group. Explain to students that they will use a thesaurus to find a more sophisticated word for each word on the list. Each new word they find must have at least three syllables. The first group that is done should stand silently. Check their answers. The first group to complete the list correctly wins. The winning group reads their words aloud for other groups to check against.

⭐ 26 ⭐
Acrostics

Materials

sidewalk chalk

Directions

Working in pairs, have each student write his or her partner's name vertically on the pavement. Tell students to use each letter of their partner's name to write an adjective that describes that person. Explain to students that they are only to write positive attributes of their partner. Students can work together to think of words that perfectly suit that person.

P oetic
A thletic
T alented

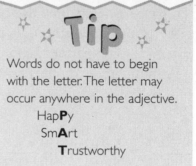

Tip
Words do not have to begin with the letter. The letter may occur anywhere in the adjective.
Hap**P**y
Sm**A**rt
Trustworthy

⭐ 27 ⭐
Adjective Art Collaborative Book

Materials

paper, colored pens or pencils

Directions

To help students understand that adjectives describe, invite them to draw and decorate the letters in an adjective to look like the adjective's meaning. Show them examples like the ones here. Ask each student to create an example of adjective art. Compile their illustrations to make a class book.

✦28✦
Comparisons

Materials

three snack items for students to compare, such as candy, pretzels, and crackers; drawing paper; crayons or markers

Directions

Remind students that the comparative form of an adjective compares two people, places, or things (e.g., A snail is slower than a crab.). The superlative form of an adjective compares more than

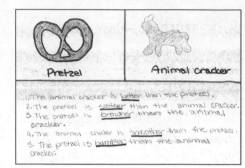

two people, places, or things (e.g., Tracy is the fastest.). For certain adjectives, the words *more* and *most* must be used (e.g, He is the more playful kitten. That necklace is the most magnificent of all.).

Have students fold the paper in half. Distribute three snack items for students to compare. On one side of the paper, have students draw two of the snacks and write five sentences to compare them. Have them underline the comparative adjectives in their sentences. Then have the students repeat the activity on the back of the paper comparing the three snacks. Have them underline the superlative adjectives in their sentences. Let students share their sentences in small groups.

Variation

◆ Tell students to imagine they are in a store shopping for an article of clothing. Let them illustrate two pieces of clothing to compare, using comparative adjectives. (E.g., This sweater is *prettier* than that one. This sweater is *redder* than that one.) Have them illustrate a third item to compare, using superlative adjectives.

✦29✦
Monster Exchange

Materials

drawing paper folded in half, notebook paper, markers, pencils

Directions

Have each student draw and color a simple monster picture on the inside half of a sheet of drawing paper. Then, on notebook paper, have the student write instructions on how to draw the monster.

Have students exchange instructions and pictures with a partner. Make sure the original monster

drawing is not showing. Each partner now must follow the instructions to draw the same monster. Once their drawings are complete, they should compare them to the original drawing on the folded paper.

Instructions and drawings are returned to the original writer so that he or she may revise the instructions to make them clearer. Discuss with students how adjectives can be used to add details.

The next day, pass the revised instructions to different students. Have that student follow the instructions to draw the monster. Let students compare the new drawings to the originals.

30
A Party Invitation

Materials

preprinted decorated bond paper, paper with a computer-generated border, or student-decorated paper

Directions

Tell students to imagine they are throwing a dinner party. Have them spend time planning the menu before they work on their invitations. Tell students they must use adjectives to describe the foods they will be serving at the party. Have students complete their invitations. Have students underline the adjectives used in each invitation. Display the invitations.

Tip

You may wish to have students vote on the best invitation and, with help from parents, prepare the feast for a classroom party.

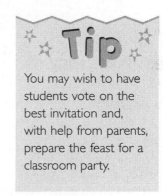

Adverbs

An **adverb** is a word that modifies or describes a verb, an adjective, or another adverb. It can tell when, where, or how

When?	Where?	How?
I **always** brush my teeth after dinner.	Juliette looked **everywhere** for her dog.	Uncle Lu held the baby **gently**.
Manuel went to the movies **yesterday**.	Take the escalator **up** to the second floor.	Walk **carefully** across the muddy field.
I will **never** forget your name.	The eagle looked **down** from the cliff.	The morning sun shines **brightly**.
There was a big storm _____ .	The bus stops _____ .	She _____ skated across the ice.
_____ _____ .	_____ _____ .	_____ _____ .
_____ _____ .	_____ _____ .	_____ _____ .
_____ _____ .	_____ _____ .	_____ _____ .
_____ _____ .	_____ _____ .	_____ _____ .

Brainstorm!

Materials

newspapers, old magazines, scissors, glue, construction paper

Directions

Working in teams, have students look through old newspapers and magazines to find examples of adverbs. Have them cut out the adverbs and glue them to construction paper. Have each group find as many examples as they can of adverbs that modify verbs, that modify adjectives, and that modify other adverbs. After 15 minutes, have teams share their findings with the whole group. The team that finds the most adverbs wins.

Variation

◆ Have students find examples of adverbs that tell how, where, and when. Have them create three brainstormed lists by gluing the words under each heading.

32

Word Search

Materials

grid paper, pencils, or puzzle-maker software or puzzle-maker Web site

Directions

Have each student generate a list of 15 adverbs. Tell students to use the grid paper and random letters to make a word search puzzle that contains their 15 words hidden vertically, horizontally, or diagonally in the puzzle. (Or, have them input the words into a puzzle-maker program that generates a puzzle.) Let students exchange puzzles.

Tip

You can have students solve the puzzle with a base word list. Students needing a challenge may enjoy solving the puzzle without a base word list.

{33}
Where? How? When?

Materials

chalkboard; three laminated index cards with the words *Where?*, *How?*, *When?*

Directions

Give the index cards to a student who acts as the Questioner. Write a simple action sentence on the board, such as *The bird sings*. Have the Questioner hold up one card and ask the question. Let a volunteer write the sentence using one or more adverbs. Volunteers in turn answer each of the three questions. Then, a new Questioner is selected and play continues with a new sentence.
Example:

How? The bird sings brightly.
Where? The bird sings here.
When? Yesterday the bird sang.

{34}
Adverb Acrostics

Materials

drawing paper, markers

Directions

Have each student write the name of a friend or family member in a vertical row down the side of the paper. Have them write adverbial phrases (a verb and adverb) for each letter of the person's name. Display the acrostics on a bulletin board.

mdstudent on `md-fsrv1\md-stud`

35

Adjective to Adverb

Materials

reproducible on page 58

Directions

Distribute the Adjective to Adverb Reproducible to pairs of students. Explain to students that they should rewrite each sentence that contains an adjective so that it now contains at least one adverb. You may wish to do the first sentence as a group.

   Tomas Garza was a careful assistant.
   Tomas Garza assisted carefully.

   Students can check one another's work in small groups.

Variation

◆ Let students write their own sentences to exchange with a partner.

36

Walking Charades

Materials

reproducible on page 59 cut into word cards, bag or box, timer

Directions

Divide students into two teams. Explain that the first player on a team draws a card from the box. He or she has one minute to act out the verb *walk* in the style of the adverb. The player cannot speak but can use props. The player's team must guess the adverb in the allotted time. Teams alternate turns until every member has had at least one chance to act. The team with the most words guessed correctly wins.

Variations

◆ Let students add their own adverb word cards.

◆ Repeat the activity using a different verb than walking (e.g., sitting or writing).

37
Tear It Up

Materials

one index card per student

Directions

Explain to students that they are going to tear their index card in half, but first they have to think about *how* they might tear it. Each student should write on the index card an adverb that describes the verb *tear*. For example, a student might write *quietly* or *carefully*. Then, one by one, let each student read his or her adverb and then tear the index card in the manner they described.

38
Noun/Verb/Adverb Mini-Book

Materials

reproducible on page 60, scissors, pencils, stapler

Directions

Have students write the subject of a sentence in the first box of a panel on the Mini-Book reproducible. Have them write a present tense verb in the second box and an adverb in the third box.
Example:

An elephant	walks	heavily.

Have students write similar sentences in the rest of the boxes.

Tell students to cut apart the panels along the dotted lines and place them in a neat stack. Have them staple along the top edge of the stack to create a mini-book. Then have them cut along the solid lines between the noun, verb, and adverb sections. Be sure they do not cut all the way to the stapled edge or the pages will come apart.

Let students flip the noun, verb, and adverb sections to create silly new sentences. Working in pairs, let students read their silly sentences aloud.

39
Interview

Materials

paper, pencils

Directions

Pair students who do not know each other very well. One student acts as the interviewer. That student asks questions to determine his or her partner's talent (or something he or she knows how to do). Remind students to use *who, what, when, where,* and *why* questions. Have the interviewer write a sentence that tells about the partner's talent. Make sure students include a minimum of one adverb in the sentence. Students then switch roles.

Each pair of students reads the sentences to the class. The class identifies the adverb used in the sentence.

40
How You Say It

Materials

paper and pencil or a computer, tape recorder (optional)

Directions

Explain to students that a radio play is performed with voices. In small groups, have students write a short radio play. You may want to use this activity to reinforce understanding of an event in history or a piece of literature your class is reading. As groups write their plays, tell them to use adverbs to give directions to the actors. Example:

Guide shouts loudly: Put the wagons in a circle. We'll make camp here for the night.

Boy cries softly: I think we're lost. When will we get there? I want to go back to Indiana.

Guide says happily: We're right on course. We'll be in our new home in two days!

Let each group record their radio play. Play the tapes for all to hear, or let students listen to them independently in a listening station.

Interjections and Conjunctions

An **interjection** is a word that expresses strong emotion.
A **conjunction** is a word that is used to join words or groups of words.

The following is a list of examples of interjections and conjunctions.
Complete the list with your own interjections and conjunctions.

INTERJECTIONS	CONJUNCTIONS
Oh!	and
Stop!	or
Wow!	either
_____	_____
_____	_____
_____	_____
_____	_____
_____	_____

☆41☆

Treasure Hunt

Materials

newspaper articles that are appropriate for children, highlighters

Directions

Enlarge each newspaper article on a photocopy machine. Have students work in pairs or small groups. Explain to students that they are on a treasure hunt to find conjunctions. Tell them to highlight each conjunction they find in the newspaper articles. Have them keep a tally chart for each word they find.

Example:

and	but	or	neither
卌												

Then provide small prizes or privileges for winners in the following categories: Most Conjunctions Found, Most Unusual Conjunction Found, Most "Ands" Found.

☆42☆

Tic-Tac-Toe

Materials

reproducible on page 53

Directions

Distribute a *Tic-Tac-Toe* reproducible to pairs of students. Explain to students that instead of using Xs and Os, one student will use interjections and one will use conjunctions. For example, the first player writes a conjunction in one square on the grid. The second player writes an interjection in another square on the grid. The first player to write three in a row—across, up and down, or diagonally—is the winner. Students should check each other's word choices.

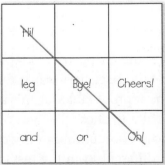

Hi!

Materials

word cards with the following words: *excited, worried, sad, surprised, bored, happy, scared, sleepy, serious*

Directions

Have a student draw a word card and say "Hi" so that it expresses the feeling described on the card. Let students take turns being the actor.

Conjunction Use

Materials

wipe-off boards, markers, tissue

Directions

Have students work in pairs. Each pair should write a sentence using a conjunction from the completed list on page 32. When students have completed one sentence, they should hold up their board and read it to the class. Check to see that they have used the word correctly. Repeat with each conjunction on the list.

Crazy About Cartoons

Materials

reproducible on page 54, scissors, tagboard, glue or tape, colored pencils, newspaper comic strips

Directions

Distribute a copy of the *Movie Frames* reproducible to each student. Have students cut the two strips from the bottom of the page and attach them to tagboard or construction paper. They will not use the stage portion of the reproducible for this activity. Display comic strip examples and discuss the format of using word bubbles to show dialogue. Tell students to make their own comic strips in the frames. Encourage them to use a minimum of two interjections in their dialogue. Have students write all interjections in a color different from the rest of the dialogue. Display the comic strips for all students to read.

Prepositions

A **preposition** is a word that relates a noun or a pronoun to another word in the sentence.

The following is a list of examples of prepositions. Example phrases are given for each preposition. Complete the list with your own prepositional phrases.

under the sea

across the street

in Boise, Idaho

about Strider's size

before _____

up _____

with _____

_____

_____

_____

_____

46

Can You Hear It?

Materials

story to read aloud, paper, pencils

Directions

Find a book or article that has a number of prepositional phrases. As you read it aloud, have students list the prepositional phrases they hear. You may wish to make it a competition to see who identifies the most.

47

Up, Down, Over, and Under

Materials

objects to hide, paper, pencils

Directions

In small groups, have students hide common objects in the classroom. Then they should write six prepositional phrases as clues to the location of the hidden object. The groups that don't hide an object follow the clues to find the object. Groups take turns writing and following clues.

48

Add it Where?

Materials

colored chalk

Directions

On the board, write a simple sentence such as *The car raced*. Call on a student to add a prepositional phrase to the beginning of the sentence, in a different color. Then have a volunteer add a prepositional phrase, using a third color, to the middle or the end of the sentence. Make sure every student has

an opportunity to edit a sentence by adding colorful prepositional phrases.
Example: <u>Over the hill</u> the car <u>in the lead</u> raced <u>toward the finish line</u>.
Here are some other simple sentences you can use:

We got lost.	I see my keys.
Maria came home.	The lizard sunned.

What Do You See?

Materials

recording of classical music, reproduction of fine art painting

Directions

To set the mood, play classical music as you display the painting. Have students write prepositional phrases that describe what they see in the painting.

For example, if you show a print of *A Sunday on La Grande Jatte* by Georges Seurat, students might list:

under an umbrella	by the water	toward the water
on the grass	in the shade	

Variation

◆ Have students write phrases while looking at an abstract painting.

Poetic Ideas

Materials

drawing paper, crayons or colored pencils

Directions

Have students decide on a topic to write about. (You may wish to suggest a topic such as a favorite animal, or a topic you have been studying in class.) Have students write a series of prepositional phrases to make a poem about the topic. The poem should begin and end with the name of the topic. Have them illustrate their poems.

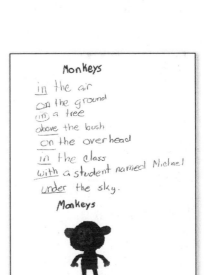

Monkeys
in the air
on the ground
in a tree
above the bush
on the overhead
in the class
with a student named Michael
under the sky.
Monkeys

Pronouns

A **pronoun** is a word that is used in place of a noun.
A **singular pronoun** names one person or thing.
A **plural pronoun** names more than one person or thing.
A **possessive pronoun** is used to show ownership or possession.

The following is a list of examples of kinds of pronouns. Example sentences are given for the pronouns. Complete the list with your own sentences.

Singular	Plural	Possessive
I, me **I** like to ice skate. Kari skates with **me**.	we, us **We** do our homework together. Would you like to study with **us**?	my, mine, our ours That is **my** book. That book is **mine**. **Our** class is reading silently. _____
you _____	you _____ _____	your, yours **Your** hat is here. **Yours** must be that one.
he, him _____ The shoe fits **him**. _____	they, them **They** are invited to the show. Invite **them**, too.	theirs _____
she, her _____ _____	they, them _____ _____	theirs _____ _____
it _____	they, them _____ _____	it _____

51
Brainstorm!

Materials

newspapers, old magazines, scissors, glue

Directions

Working in pairs, have students look through old newspapers and magazines to find examples of pronouns. Have them cut out the pronouns and glue them to chart paper. Have each pair find two examples each of a singular, plural, and possessive pronoun. Once each group has contributed six pronouns, review the words with the whole class to determine that each word is an example of a pronoun.

52
I Know That Story!

Materials

simple picture book with words

Directions

Explain to students that you will read them a story. Tell them to listen for pronouns in the story. When they hear a pronoun, they should raise their hands.

Variation

◆ Have students identify what noun the pronoun is taking the place of.

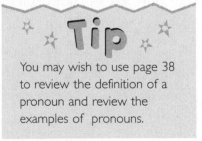

Tip

You may wish to use page 38 to review the definition of a pronoun and review the examples of pronouns.

39

Who Am I?

Materials

paper, pencils

Directions

Ask students to list pronouns that can be used to replace their names. Let each student choose one pronoun from the list to use in a sentence. As they say the pronoun, list it on the board or chart paper. Have students use the definitions on page 38 to determine what kinds of pronouns were listed (singular pronouns). Once the activity is completed, add other pronouns.

Pronoun Bee

Materials

list of sentences (see samples below)

Directions

Divide students into two teams. Have teams stand on opposite sides of the room as if they were in a Spelling Bee. Read a sentence to the first player. Have the student repeat the sentence replacing a noun with a pronoun. (They can choose whatever noun they wish if the sentence contains more than one.) Play continues, eliminating players who miss. The object is to keep as many players standing as possible.

Example sentences:

Saundra lives on a farm. (_She_ lives on a farm.)

Phillip and Amy like to paint. (_They_ like to paint.)

Hold the flower in your hand. (Hold _it_ in your hand.)

Micah and I ate lunch. (_We_ ate lunch.)

This is my pen. (This is _mine_.)

I have John's jacket. (I have _his_ jacket.)

Don't sit on Mom and Dad's car. (Don't sit on _their_ car.)

I or Me?

Materials

reproducible of page 61 as an overhead transparency, two index cards per person, markers

Directions

Have students write *ME* on one index card and *I* on the other. Place the reproducible on the overhead with only the first sentence displayed (cover the rest of the overhead with a sheet of paper). Have students choose the correct response to complete each sentence by holding up the appropriate index card.

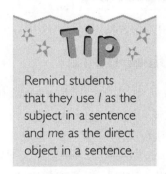

Tip

Remind students that they use *I* as the subject in a sentence and *me* as the direct object in a sentence.

56

"Choose the Correct Pronoun" Game

Materials

wipe-off boards and markers, reproducible on page 62 as an overhead transparency

Directions

Display the transparency on an overboard. Cover all except the first sentence. Read the sentence and have students write the correct pronoun on a wipe-off board or a sheet of paper. Then, reveal the answer. Discuss why the answer is correct. Each student scores a point for a correct answer. Students wipe off their boards and continue the activity for each sentence. Make up a funny point spread for the game. For example,

    Points
    7–8   **YOU** are a pronoun!
    4–6   **I** wish I knew more about pronouns!
    1–3   **WE** need to study pronouns!

Variation

◆ Copy one reproducible for each pair of students. Students play the game with a partner.

57
Can This Be Homework?

Materials

paper, pencil, television program

Directions

Tell students that their homework assignment is to watch ten minutes of television. They may wish to use a timer to keep track of the ten-minute interval. As they watch the program, they should record any pronouns they hear. They should tally each pronoun to determine which one was used the most.

The next day, have students share their data with the class. Discuss with students what pronouns were used the most.

Variation

◆ Tape ten-minute segments from a variety of programs. In class, have students watch the tape and tally the use of pronouns.

58
Pronoun Bingo

Materials

reproducible on page 56, markers such as beans or buttons,
list of 25 pronouns on chart paper or the board (see below)

Directions

Distribute one copy of the reproducible to each student. Display the list of 25 pronouns. Instruct students to fill in the spaces on their *Bingo* cards, in any order, with the pronouns. Possible pronouns:

he	she	you	they	it	him	her	your	them
its	his	hers	our	their	anybody	nobody	itself	himself
herself	yourself	us	we	me	I	mine		

Then, say a fill-in-the-blank sentence to the class. As you read, students place a marker on the pronoun that would complete the sentence correctly. The first player to score five words in a row— horizontally, vertically, or diagonally—wins the game. Be sure to check students' work to be sure they chose the correct pronoun to complete the sentence.

☆59☆

What Did You Do Last Night?

Directions

To help students understand the importance of pronouns in our language, ask them to think about something they did last evening. Call on a volunteer to describe the event. Then ask the student to repeat the story *without* using any pronouns. Let volunteers take turns telling their stories in this way.

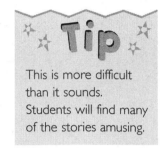

Tip

This is more difficult than it sounds. Students will find many of the stories amusing.

☆60☆

Replace Me

Materials

books of poetry and nursery rhymes

Directions

Working in groups, have students search through books to find lines of poetry that include nouns. Have them write the lines on a paper, leaving two or three blank lines between each line of poetry. Once students have their lines of poetry, have them replace the nouns in each line with pronouns. Then students exchange papers with another group. On the third line under each line of poetry, have them replace the pronouns with new nouns. They may make silly sentences.

For example,

1. Mary had a little lamb.
2.
3.

1. Mary had a little lamb.
2. <u>She</u> had <u>her</u>.
3.

1. Mary had a little lamb.
2. <u>She</u> had <u>her</u>.
3. Ms. Wong had a baby girl.

1. Little Jack Horner sat in a corner.
2.
3.

1. Little Jack Horner sat in a corner.
2. <u>He</u> sat in <u>it</u>.
3.

1. Little Jack Horner sat in a corner.
2. <u>He</u> sat in <u>it</u>.
3. The principal sat in a bowl of oatmeal.

Sentences

The essential elements of a sentence are the **subject** and the **predicate**. The **subject** names a person, place, or a thing about which a statement is made. It tells who or what the statement is about.

The **predicate** tells something about the subject. It describes what the subject is doing.

The following is a list of examples of sentences that have been divided into subjects and predicates. Complete the list with your own subjects and predicates.

SUBJECT	PREDICATE
My pen	fell.
The teacher	sneezed.
The big round moon	shines brightly.
The Wizard of Oz	hid behind the curtain.
_____	hops on one foot.
_____	slipped.
A tiny insect	_____.
Those shoes	_____.
_____	_____.
_____	_____.

61

Sentence or Fragment?

Directions

Read, one by one, a list of examples of complete sentences and fragments (see below). Tell students to determine whether they hear a sentence or a fragment. If it is a complete sentence, they should hold up both arms and give a silent cheer. If it is a fragment, they should give a thumbs-down sign.
Examples:

> Ran fast across the finish line.
> The opera singer hit a high note.
> The large yellow sunflower and the small red tulip.
> The painter splashed paint onto the floor.
> The plane landed.
> Slowly the long freight train chugged to a stop at the platform.
> Children in France and Italy.
> Caught the basketball.

62

Round Robin

Directions

Take the class outdoors and sit in a circle. Begin the game by naming a subject you can see, such as *Small, chirping birds*. Have the student sitting beside you give a predicate to complete the subject, such as *are eating birdseed from the feeder*. This makes the complete sentence *Small, chirping birds are eating birdseed from the feeder*. Play continues with the next student in the circle beginning a sentence with a subject. Each player in turns says a subject or predicate to make complete sentences.

Variation

◆ Play the same game with related sentences that form a story.

Sentence Building

Materials

reproducible on page 63, pencils

Directions

Distribute the *Sentence Building* reproducible to each student. Assign students a theme, such as community, the rain forest, volcanoes, or a familiar folk tale. Have them write examples in each column. Then have students exchange papers with a partner. The partner selects one example from each column to make sentences. Once the partner has made five sentences, students students read their new sentences aloud.

	Fun with Grammar · Scholastic Professional Books			
Name			Date	
	Reproducible			
Sentence Building				
Who? (subject)	**What?** (verb)	**When?** (adverb)	**Where?** (object)	**Why?** (prepositional phrase)

Tip

Some sentences will be silly. Correct any incomplete sentences formed.

Your Turn

Materials

wipe-off boards, markers

Directions

Have students work in pairs. Have one student write a simple subject on paper. Then have the partner write a funny simple predicate for the subject. Continue by having students take turns writing sentences that include the following:

compound subjects   compound predicates
complete subjects   complete predicates
compound subjects and compound predicates
complete subjects and complete predicates

Let partners choose their best three sentences to share with the class. Have them identify what type of subject and predicate is in each sentence.

65

Occupations

Materials

paper, pencils, timer

Directions

Talk briefly with students about occupations available to them in the future. Then set a timer for five minutes. Tell students that during the allotted time they should write sentences that contain simple subjects and coordinating simple predicates that tell about occupations. They can only use a subject once and a predicate once. Examples: Writers create. Athletes train. Teachers inspire.

When their lists are complete, have them exchange papers with a partner to check each other's capitalization, punctuation, and sentence sense. You may wish to count to see who produced the most sentences.

66

Story Builders

Materials

index cards, magazines, catalogs, scissors, glue or tape

Directions

Let students look through old magazines, catalogs, and advertisements to cut out small objects to glue onto index cards. They should find a variety of pictures. Once cards are complete, shuffle them and deal five to each player. Cards are left face down. The first player turns over a card. For example, he or she may turn over a picture of a plate. The player begins the story by telling a complete sentence that includes a reference to a plate. The sentence can be serious, realistic, or silly, but it must be complete.

Tip

Laminate the cards to make them more durable. These can also be used again the following year.

Example:

One spring morning, Plate sat up on the shelf knowing that he'd no longer live his life lying down.
Then the second player turns over his or her top card. It is a picture of a swimming pool.
Plate rolled into the park and threw himself into the cool blue swimming pool water.
The third player draws a card and continues the story, including a picture of a doll into the story.
The story telling continues until all the cards have been used.

Parts of Speech Review

A **noun** is a word that names a person, place, thing, or idea. A noun can act or be acted upon.

A **verb** is a word that shows action, being, or a state of being.

An **adjective** is a word that modifies or describes a noun or a pronoun. It can tell what kind, how many, or which one.

An **adverb** is a word that modifies or describes a verb, an adjective, or another adverb. It can tell when, where, or how.

An **interjection** is a word that expresses strong emotion.

A **conjunction** is a word that is used to join words or groups of words.

A **preposition** is a word that relates a noun or a pronoun to another word in the sentence.

A **pronoun** is a word that is used in place of a noun.

67

Scavenger Hunt

Materials

newspapers, magazines, paper, pencils, glue, scissors

Directions

Have each student fold a sheet of paper into eight equal sections. Have students label each section with a part of speech: *noun, verb, adjective, adverb, interjection, conjunction, preposition, pronoun.* Students then search through old newspapers and magazines to find at least two examples of each part of speech to glue into each section. Have partners check each other's work.

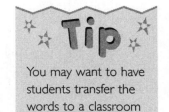

Tip

You may want to have students transfer the words to a classroom chart to use in their writing activities.

68

Parts of Speech Race

Materials

50–100 index cards, open space (such as a gymnasium or playground)

Directions

Tip
This game may be played by a small group, large group, or whole class. Monitor the Caller to make sure he or she uses a variety of parts of speech and numbers.

Have students write high-frequency, commonly used, or vocabulary words (one word per card) on index cards. Make sure the cards are a representative assortment of the parts of speech (noun, verb, adjective, adverb, interjection, conjunction, preposition, pronoun).

Designate a student to be the Caller. The Caller shuffles and distributes one word card to each player. Students stand around the Caller in a large semicircle. Each player must be an equal distance from the Caller. The Caller faces away from the players. The Caller names a part of speech and a number between one and four. Players look at the word on their card. If it is an example of the part of speech the Caller named, the Player calls out the word and steps forward the number steps named by the Caller. (Beforehand, demonstrate that a "step" occurs when the heel of one foot is placed in front of the toe of the other foot.) When a player is close enough, he or she taps the Caller on the shoulder. This player now becomes the Caller. The cards are collected and shuffled and a new round begins.

69

Find It

Materials

16 index cards for each pair of students, markers

Directions

On eight of the index cards have students print the parts of speech (one word per card) *noun, verb, adjective, adverb, interjection, conjunction, preposition, pronoun.* On the other eight cards have students print one example of each part of speech.

Pairs of students shuffle the cards and set them facedown in a four-by-four grid. The first player turns over any two cards. If the two cards match (such as *noun, flower*), the player keeps the cards and his or her play continues until the two cards turned over do not match. Each player in turn continues until all cards are matched. The player who has formed the most pairs wins.

70

Parts of Speech Bingo

Materials

reproducible on page 56, markers such as beans or buttons

Directions

Distribute one copy of the *Bingo* reproducible to each student. Display a list of 25 vocabulary words (the list should have five each of five parts of speech you wish to reinforce). Instruct students to fill in the spaces on their *Bingo* cards, in any order, with the words. Possible words:

Nouns	Verbs	Adverbs	Pronouns	Prepositions
leg	climb	quickly	she	of
butterfly	crawl	never	it	over
Anita	love	forever	you	across
Boston	read	honestly	I	below
joy	break	loudly	his	before

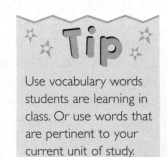

Tip

Use vocabulary words students are learning in class. Or use words that are pertinent to your current unit of study.

Then, name a part of speech to the class, such as *pronoun*. As you read, students place a marker on a word on their board that is a pronoun (for example, *she*, *it*, *you*, *I*, or *his*). Do not name a part of speech more than five times. The first player to score five words in a row—horizontally, vertically, or diagonally—wins the game. Check students' work to be sure they covered words that are the parts of speech you named.

71

Don't Say It

Materials

cards with the following parts of speech: *noun, proper noun, verb, adjective, adverb, interjection, conjunction, preposition.*

Directions

One student is chosen to be the Don't-Say-It tester. He or she draws a card from the pile. Then the student goes around the room asking questions that try to trick the other players into saying that part of speech. If asked a question, the student in the audience must answer. The player who uses the designated part of speech is eliminated. Then another player takes a turn as the Don't-Say-It tester. The game continues until all players are eliminated.

⭐72⭐
Categories

Materials

reproducible on page 53, timer, pencils

Directions

Name four parts of speech to have students write at the top of each
column on the *Categories* reproducible. Then, choose five letters for
them to write in the first column. Explain to students that they should
try to fill in the grid with words that are examples of that part of
speech and start with the letter in the first column. Set a timer for five
minutes. When time is up, let students share answers in small groups.
Encourage students to give unusual or unique answers.

Tip

Categories can be
played by individuals,
pairs, small groups, or
the whole class.

⭐73⭐
My Acrostic

Materials

paper, pencils

Directions

Have each student write his or her name vertically on paper. Tell students to use each letter of
their name to write a certain part of speech that describes or is associated with themselves.
Example:

	Noun	Verb	Adjective
P	person	practices	pretty
A	athlete	acts	accurate
M	monitor	makes	mysterious

Variation

◆ You could use all or any of the parts of speech in this activity.

☆ 74 ☆
Superstar!

Materials

markers, yellow construction paper, glue

Directions

Have students draw a star on the construction paper. Explain that they are each a superstar, and they are to follow these directions to write a self-description:

Line 1: four adjectives that describe you

Line 2: four nouns that refer to you (for example, *friend, cousin*)

Line 3: three interjections that you say

Line 4: four verbs that tell things that you can do

Line 5: one sentence about yourself that has a conjunction

Line 6: two prepositional phrases that tell where you can usually be found

Have students write the description on the star and cut it out.

Tip

Hole punch one of the star points and run yarn through it to hang the stars from the ceiling.

Variation

◆ Students may wish to add a self-portrait or small photo of themselves to the back of the star.

☆ 75 ☆

Story Completion

Materials

reproducible on page 64

Directions

Distribute the *Story Completion* reproducible to pairs of students. One student acts as the Writer. The partner acts as the Parts of Speech Expert. The Writer asks the Parts of Speech Expert for an example of a part of speech to fill in each blank. The Writer fills in each answer. Then the Writer reads the completed story aloud.

Variation

◆ Let students write their own Story Completions to try with one another.

Reproducible

Tic-Tac-Toe

Categories

Letter				

Reproducible

Movie Frames

Reproducible

Once Upon a Time

Complete the story with adjectives.

The _____ Duckling

Once upon a time on a/an _____ farm, there lived a duck family. Mother Duck had been sitting on _____ eggs. One _____ morning, the eggs hatched and out popped _____ _____ ducklings. But _____ duckling was _____ than the rest.

"I can't understand how this _____ duckling can be one of mine!" Mother Duck said to herself, shaking her head. As the days went by, the _____ duckling became more and more _____ . His brothers didn't want to play with him because he was so _____ . He felt _____ and _____ , while Mother Duck did her best to console him.

"Poor _____ , _____ duckling!" she would say. "Why are you so different from the others?" And the _____ duckling felt worse than ever.

One day at dawn, he ran away from the _____ farmyard. He stopped at a pond and questioned _____ birds. "Do you know of any ducklings with _____ feathers like mine?"

They replied, "We don't know anyone as _____ as you." The _____ duckling did not lose heart however, and kept making inquiries. He went to the _____ pond, where _____ geese gave him the same answer. They warned him, "Don't stay here! It's dangerous. There are men with _____ guns around here!"

He fled as far away as he could and hid in a _____ bed of reeds.

One day, he saw a group of _____ birds overhead. They were _____ , with _____ , _____ necks, _____ bills, and _____ wings.

"If only I could look like them," said the duckling. "Then someone would love me." Winter came and the water froze. The _____ duckling went in search of food. He dropped to the ground exhausted. A _____ farmer found him and put him in his _____ pocket.

"I'll take him home. _____ thing, he's frozen!" The _____ duckling was able to survive the _____ , _____ winter at the _____ farm.

Soon he had grown so big that the farmer freed him by the _____ pond.

That was when the duckling saw himself mirrored in the water.

"How I've changed! What am I?" A group of swans landed nearby.

"You're a swan like us!" they said. "Where have you been hiding?"

"It's a _____ story," replied the no-longer _____ duckling. He swam majestically with the _____ swans. He heard children on the riverbank exclaim, "Look at that _____ swan! He's the finest of them all!"

Reproducible

Bingo Board

Reproducible

I Can Beat That Word

Write a sophisticated synonym for each word. Your new word must have at least three syllables.

pretty _____	nice _____
mean _____	little _____
red _____	some _____
big _____	scary _____
kind _____	cute _____
blue _____	funny _____
good _____	sad _____
bad _____	happy _____
old _____	new _____
ugly _____	dirty _____
easy _____	cool _____
great _____	brown _____

Reproducible

Adjective to Adverb

Rewrite each sentence so it contains at least one adverb.

1. Tomas Garza was a careful assistant.

_____

2. That is a playful kitten.

_____

3. The quick blue car raced around the track.

_____

4. The heavy snow caused school to be canceled.

_____

5. She looked at her sad face in the mirror.

_____

6. Ms. Johnson is a speedy skater.

_____

7. The secret letter was slipped under the door.

_____

8. Tran felt nervous singing on the stage.

_____

Reproducible

Walking Charades

quietly	quickly
happily	clumsily
aristocratically	watchfully
calmly	awkwardly
timidly	sadly
sleepily	nervously

Reproducible

Mini-Book

Reproducible

I or Me?

1. Juan and _____ are going to the movies on Friday night.

2. Sarah said that Dimetry and _____ won the contest!

3. Please give the finished drawings to _____ .

4. Why is it that Molly can't go with _____ ?

5. Someone told Christina and _____ about the surprise party.

6. The teacher walked with Chase and _____ to the cafeteria.

7. My friends and _____ would like to attend the dance recital.

8. Lauren and _____ gave the puppy to Hailey.

9. _____ am going to take guitar lessons.

10. The calico cat followed _____ .

Reproducible

Choose the Correct Pronoun

Choose the correct pronoun to complete each sentence.

1. Give (he, him) the book.

2. Hector and (he, him) are working together.

3. Two of her sisters and (she, her) will do the job.

4. Give the pen to (her, she) right now.

5. I took the lasagna from (she, her).

6. Abdul and (he, him) play basketball.

7. John and (me, I) are going to the movies on Saturday.

8. The gifts were given to Sarah and (we, us) after the presentation.

9. Darnel and (he, him) left class early.

10. Alex walked (her, she) all the way home.

Reproducible

Sentence Building

Who? (subject)	What? (verb)	When? (adverb)	Where? (object)	Why? (prepositional phrase)

Reproducible

Story Completion

Yesterday, our class went on a trip to the zoo. It is across the street from

the _____. I couldn't wait to see the _____. When I
      noun (place)   noun (animal)

last went to the zoo _____ , the _____ were
                     prepositional phrase (tells when)   plural noun (animal)

_____ and _____ . The _____ one
   verb (-ing)   verb (-ing)   comparative adjective

looked _____ at me. Even though all that happened, I still wanted
          adverb (ly)

to go back.

     I walked through the zoo gates and said, "_____ !" I couldn't
                                                    interjection

believe how the place had changed. Where the _____ used to be
                                              noun (plural)

were now _____ . The new zoo was much better than the old one!
            noun (plural)

_____ and I _____ over to the monkey area.
  proper noun (person)   action verb (past tense)

_____ said, "_____ , I've never seen a monkey
     pronoun   interjection

_____ ."
 verb (present tense)

     We walked on and saw _____ _____ and
                               adjective   plural noun (animal)

_____ _____ _____ . It was the
  adjective   plural noun (animal)   verb (ing)

_____ thing we saw all day!
 superlative adjective

     I love the zoo!

64